Fatale Requiem

Emma Hernandez

BookLeaf
Publishing

India | USA | UK

Presentation by *BookLeaf Publishing*

Web: www.bookleafpub.com

E-mail: info@bookleafpub.com

ISBN: 9789363303232

First edition 2024

Season of Death

Dry branches, bleak skies
No second chances
To say my goodbyes

Frigid winds blow with ice bound blades
Every cutting edge penetrates

Whilst painting each crease of mine cracked skin
With crimson droplets so thin,
for tears of droughty eyes never begin

Picking me apart, I felt not a pain nor the
happiness that came
No breath of life left in my heart, its beating left
in vain,
Leastways I have mine slit skin to cry for my
now loveless self
Save thine false sympathies for the far end of the
shelf

No need to spare a single breath
In this season of death

Spring Day

Though the threads that kept warmth to my heart
has fallen apart
A spring day arrives after the barren winter does
depart
The time of revival for those lost that ever died
so young
  either bloom or transform once again
  before a breath could escape thy tongue
And as the four winds do continue their cycle,
  as the seasons change just as people do,
  the longer I remain
  the more my mind doth derange
And no matter what change
Entranced by an existence of something
Will disappear with consistence into nothing

Solemn Orisons

To our Lord which art in heaven,
Most certainly hallowed be thy name
Hear a sinners call without thy blame
And let it be this once
   that you hear my selfish plea
   in the midst of this forsaken eve
   lift me out of the bottomless sea
I beg of you please,
Lend me what my heart yearns for

For ahead I see before me
A fair maiden bright and bare
Of whom I could not help but stare
And hear of her resounding voice
   amplifying the background lair
   sounding much like winter bells so joyous
   of matters so frivolous she cheerfully tells
   with doe eyed listeners surround

To our Lord who art in heaven,
A terrible longing has befallen me
It being according to ye will is a lie
But continue to beg thee,
   please swap our places
   and give me her prize
   place upon me

her beautiful guise
lend me the tears
Illuminating her eyes
cover my bones with her skin so nice

To our Lord which art in heaven,
I come before thee knowing this be possible
Not as I will but as thou wilt
Use thy miracles so unstoppable
O' please,
I come before thee
  with blood on my knees
  and palms glued to the floor
  using last of my weakened resolve
  to present thee the words of my soul

And this before all:
Bestow on me not only her elegant visage
  but also the light of her heart so privileged
  so that I won't feel so picked apart
In this bottomless vacant sea
  where I know not of whether
  I so painfully sink or swim
  limb by limb,
  I need to feel human again

O' Lord who art in the highest universe
Allow my body to let my soul leave
For only this one forsaken eve

Elegy of One's Own Passing

5

Rejoice! Let the bells ring!
"Today is the youngest you'll ever be."
One may not feel a thing
For now or the morrow albeit momentary
Will it make me lesser? Can we stay together?
No matter, celebrate this now or never again

Lumi Gardelle

On this day I celebrate the arrival of dear Lumi
Avoidant eyes look through and o'er the birth of
a mob
Left with a letter on hand and returned with a
new destiny
Unrecognizable, unnoticeable, unimaginably
unamused
Hastily, she left the scene on the corduroy
No one seeing her, no one seeing me,
No one seeing in me pure visible joy
I am alone but alone I am with thee

Two outcast travelers were we before she sailed
across the sea
And finally returned but returned not to me
For a lad with more grace than me
Is the man she claimed as her true destiny
She promised me a home when mine burned to
ash and ash alone
With nothing to give, I suppose it be better to go
on my own

She killed me, my body it fell
She killed me and left with organs to sell
may it be

Doubts of the Self Assured

Lovelorn? No, not I
I know without try
that one such way I do not fly
As said before
Any stirrings in the chest
Disappear and return nevermore

Every time, as night follows the day
From me Cupid pulled their arrow away
Aside from this new thing stuck in my head
Awake all night in my bed
Their essence is filling my senses
My heart left defenseless, a new pestilence

Saying this is nothing more than senseless
But I think that this time
I yearn to call them mine

What the Stars Don't Tell You

No guiding messenger
No advanced calendar
No esteemed astrologer
  could have predicted
   the warnings of falling stars
   that could get me addicted
Never said 'would'
But perhaps I should
Nothing else could ever be
any more unexpected

The Reveal

Upon one spring's morning did I wander
into the very ends of my dreams yonder
at which before drifting into wakefulness
was when my own secrets hidden
and kept from my own awareness
did whisper sweetly, causing bareness
of my own heart to be felt
I was told that someone was the raison d'être
of the current beating of my heart
it was indeed that very feeling
this changes everything

The Unapologetic

Let me tell you about the one who dared to get
too close
The unapologetic one, giving me a hard dose
of what it felt like to appear as red as a winter
rose
Their nerve to grasp my hand, giving me that
glow
and commit such actions that weren't meant for
friend or foe
You never really meant them did you though?
Giving me those foolhardy illusions, during time
in seclusions
Why pour the warm light of special attention
upon me, the subject of your every other
mention?
As if there really were instances, slight chances
of me being a special part of what you thought
romance is

Ode to Youthful Days

I can recall all too well,
the cotton candy skies
discussions through the nights
silly banter lies
laugher by surprise
all when my longing eyes
prized your boyish guise

Dull

I remember all too well, it certainly does ring a
bell
How with you it felt so warm, but little did I
know
That if you knew it would've only fed your ego
I should have known that so long ago

You further say I was dull
When I strived to be right for you
I was a lull before the storm passed through
At the time I fell for you

Blue and Grey

If you could declare
what was wrong with me
then maybe bother appreciating
but instead you buried me plenty
under the garden you made for another being
with that infatuated feeling, I can understand
that
But the things you would say, leaving me grey
I suppose it is my fault for wanting you to stay

Corpse

Eyes on my form, pale skin being too ghastly
Hands on my arm, endless reminders of my
fragility
From my head to my toes, just skin and bones
Compared me to the walking dead, my figure
you dread
This cadaverous frame I posses is what you
scrutinize as if you obsess
And within the mess is the kindred soul you
ignored
As it peeks through each rib pair
Waiting for one to remove layer after layer with
care,
Strip it bare

Midnight Madness

In the midst of moonless nights,
As we retreat to the secrecy of our rooms,
a dark veil hides our very essence
With blissful secrecy
And one cannot help but wonder
That just around the corner
There are those who are not them
In the arms of people who are not theirs

Recipe to One's Own Destruction

Iv'e been drinking from overflowing rivers
but the body remains empty
and insatiable thirst only grows
for something that will devour me
and lately
no pure drink can satisfy me
you can call me greedy
but I have no beating heart
to know what it's like to be content
with things within my reach

This mind isn't mine or in my control
I am all I have
so forgive me for the days
that leave me dry as a weed
the flame too close to my withering self
it burns.

Birthday

Best day of the year, worst day of my life
Who knew a day of a new life, could fill decades
with strife
Future torn apart the moment the needles opened
the way
When placed in your stiffened arms, did you feel
life slip away?
Mistaken a burdened responsibility for a bundle
of joy
It wasn't my fault, It wasn't your fault
Please let me go, let me breathe
So that you can find you and not me

The friendship I elicited; by chance or mistake?

Properly secured from the world surround
Kept in my flowered pen
Built just for me by the guardian
All luxurious necessities within the inside
But I yearn to lean towards the out side
I want to see, I want to hear, I want to learn
From those who pass by the outside

Of course I'm mostly accompanied
By mellow familiars and darling playfellows
They come to say their greetings
Then they follow each other's leadings
From this little pen I love to join
But all is the same forevermore whilst not
hearing my pleadings

Not often disgraced by separations; not often
loving solitary silence
I stood to appear lofty, high enough to defy my
curse of concealment
Through evergreens and pastures a distance
ahead
A fellow strolling by, extended words wrongly
said

Ringing laughter spilled from my lips
Amusement written all over my face
A few more days of this and a friend was made
to fill the space

The world only perceivable to me, heavily
altered
Once was always the observer, always the
witness
Whispering beneath a guise of content, "why not
me"
Every time a good thing to someone came to be

Now, after nearly a decade,
it was now my turn to join the parade
I beauty of another presence ignited a light that
never died
I am at the mouth that followed it so very
closely
For without it, I'll not know which way is up
From dusk till dawn please stay till then
I'd like to see you again, friend

Not Today

Let it find me another day
the very thing looking at me
from under my skin
needles prodding at my limb
it wont be very long
until it finds me again

www.ingramcontent.com/pod-product-compliance
Lightning Source LLC
La Vergne TN
LVHW050310200726

843509LV00015B/3250